MY GIRLFRIEND'S A GEEK ❷

RIZE SHINBA
PENTABU

Translation: Stephen Paul
Lettering: Primary Graphix - John Hunt

Yen Press
Hachette Book Group
237 Park Avenue, New York, NY 10017

www.HachetteBookGroup.com
www.YenPress.com

Yen Press is an imprint of Hachette Book Group, Inc. The Yen Press name and logo are trademarks of Hachette Book Group, Inc.

First Yen Press Edition: November 2010

ISBN: 978-0-7595-3174-1

10 9 8 7 6 5 4 3 2 1

BVG

Printed in the United States of America

Wonderfully illustrated modern day crossover fantasy, available at your local bookstore or comic shop!

Apart from the fact her eyes turn red when the moon rises, Myung-Ee is your average, albeit boy-crazy, 5th grader. After picking a fight with her classmate Yu-Da Lee, she discovers a startling secret: the two of them are "earth rabbits" being hunted by the "fox tribe" of the moon!

Five years pass and Myung-Ee transfers to a new school in search of pretty boys. There, she unexpectedly reunites with Yu-Da. The problem is he doesn't remember a thing about her or their shared past!

Moon Boy

걸요일 소년

1~9 FINAL

Lee Young You

A totally new Arabian nights, where Scheherazade is a guy!

Everyone knows the story of Scheherazade and her wonderful tales from the Arabian Nights. For one thousand and one nights, the stories that she created entertained the mad Sultan and eventually saved her life. In this version, Scheherazude is a guy who disguises himself as a woman to save his sister from the mad Sultan. When he puts his life on the line, what kind of strange and unique stories will he tell? This new twist on one of the greatest classical tales might just keep you awake for another ONE THOUSAND AND ONE NIGHTS!

Yen Press
www.yenpress.com

Available at bookstores near you!

One thousand and one nights 1~11 final

Han SeungHee · Jeon JinSeok

Kieli sees ghosts.
Harvey cannot die.
He will throw
her world into
chaos...
...and become her
one true friend.

STORY BY **Yukako Kabei**
ART BY **Shiori Teshirogi**

KIELI

To become the ultimate weapon, one boy must eat the souls of 99 humans...

...and one witch.

Maka is a scythe meister, working to perfect her demon scythe until it is good enough to become Death's Weapon—the weapon used by Shinigami-sama, the spirit of Death himself. And if that isn't strange enough, her scythe also has the power to change form—into a human-looking boy!

VOLUME 4 IN STORES NOW

Yen Press
Yen Press is an imprint of
Hachette Book Group
www.yenpress.com

Soul Eater ©Atsushi Ohkubo/SQUARE ENIX

THE POWER TO RULE THE HIDDEN WORLD OF SHINOBI...

THE POWER COVETED BY EVERY NINJA CLAN...

...LIES WITHIN THE MOST APATHETIC, DISINTERESTED VESSEL IMAGINABLE.

Nabari No Ou
Yuhki Kamatani

MANGA VOLUMES 1-5 NOW AVAILABLE

The
Phantomhive
family has a butler
who's almost too
good to be true...

...or maybe
he's just too
good to be
human.

Black Butler

YANA TOBOSO

VOLUMES 1-3 IN STORES NOW!

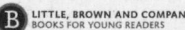

*Yen Press
cordially invites you to celebrate the*
MR. FLOWER SERIES
by Lily Hoshino!

On sale now!

GIVING THEM NAMES REALLY HELPS YOU DEVELOP AN ATTACHMENT TO THEM.

THAT'S RIGHT.

SO FIRST YOU WATCHED A MOVIE TOGETHER, THEN YOU WATCHED COPPOLA THE GOLDFISH TOGETHER?

OH, THAT COPPOLA.

HE GIVES ALL OF HIS TROPICAL FISH THE NAMES OF MOVIE DIRECTORS.

I CAN'T EVEN TELL WHICH GUPPY IS WHICH.

HMMMMM-MMMM...

KIRIRIN (SPARKLE)

WHO KNOWS WHAT COULD HAVE JUST SET HER SENSORS OFF?

HEH HEH HEH...

OH, NOTHING.

SO WHAT'S YOUR POINT!?

◆ END ◆

FRIENDLY COOPERATION, HUH?

VERY STUDIOUS OF YOU.

HMM. HMM.

WE JUST WORKED ON OUR REPORTS...

JUST SETTING THE MOOD, HEE-HEE-HEE...

THAT SOUNDS LIKE FILM CLUB TO ME!

WE WATCHED A DVD...

C-COPPOLA!?

FROM "STRAWBERRY MARSH-MALLOW"!?

YEP.

HAS HE GOTTEN BIGGER?

WE MADE SURE TO FEED COPPOLA...

UHH... SINCE WHEN DID FRANCIS FORD COPPOLA DO MOE?

HUH?

ANA COPPOLA, HUH? WHAT A SURPRISE.

SO KOUJI-KUN'S INTO THAT KIND OF MOE STUFF?

THAT'S THE NAME OF KOUJI'S BLACK MOOR GOLDFISH.

STRAW-BERRY?

162

ALL I SAID WAS...

"OHH, YOU WENT OVER TO KOUJI-KUN'S HOUSE, HUH? HMMMMM."

WHEN YOU SAY *"HMMMMMM,"* IT HAS A WEIRD NOTE OF SUGGESTION TO IT!

THAT'S ALL. NO BIGGIE.

NO, IT DOESN'T.

THAT'S IT! THAT!!

PATAN (THUMP)

YOU KNOW, THE HARDER YOU TRY TO DENY THIS, THE MORE SUSPICIOUS IT SEEMS.

CAN YOU TELL ME WHAT YOU WERE DOING THERE, ANYWAY?

WELL, IT'S NOTHING LIKE WHAT YOU'RE HOPING TO HEAR...

ARE YOU EVEN LISTENING, YUIKO-SAN!?

COME ON!

IF YOU KNOW, WOULD YOU STOP TALKING ABOUT THESE POTENTIALLY SLANDEROUS DAYDREAMS OF YOURS?

DO YOU HAVE A PERSECU-TION COMPLEX OR SOME-THING?

KOUJI'S JUST A FRIEND! WE'RE PALS, NOTHING MORE!

AND YES, I AM LISTENING.

I KNOW THAT.

YOU DON'T HAVE TO SHOUT.

MY GIRLFRIEND'S A GEEK.

THAT'S JUST HOW THE WORLD WORKS! DON'T BRING IT UP!

SHH!

THE COMIC VERSION SURE HAS ADDED A BUNCH OF EXTRA STUFF TO THE STORY.

I'D LOVE TO BE ABLE TO TRADE BARBS THE WAY PENTABU-SAN AND Y-KO-SAN ALWAYS DO, BUT I'VE STILL GOT A LONG WAY TO GO.

| | You were totally drooling over that illustration of Yuiko-san with cat ears in Volume 1 of the manga. |
| Me | ...True, because that was incredibly cute. |

To be honest, I felt that I suddenly gained a deep understanding of the concept of "moe" in that one instant.

...Beware the power of Shinba-sensei.

In one single volume, I've been awakened to the lures of not only collarbones, but cat ears! And even the realm of moe as well!

Y-ko	And that means it's worth trying out **a boy equipped with cat ears** too, isn't it?
Me	Why would it mean that!?

Y-ko **C'mon, look. Cat-eared boy!**

Me	Seriously, you don't have to show me!
Y-ko	Don't worry, babe. I understand the fear and anxiety that comes from **accidentally developing a new kink**.
Me	......What?
Y-ko	I know, I know. It's really scary to tread into uncharted territory. But don't you realize that if you stop and let the fear overtake you, humanity will never evolve to new heights?
Me	Uhh, I don't think this is a problem that deserves to be described on such a massive scale...
Y-ko	That's why I do not fear! I do not stop! After all, you never know!

What lies ahead could be something that's really damn moe!

So, honey—here's your chance! You're going to find something that surpasses even collarbones in your book!

Let's try getting into cat-eared boys!!

So anyway...
We're doing great, and life is better than ever.

Spring 2008
Pentabu
Y-ko

Y-ko	What, you can't? Fine, **Code Geass** will do. Season two's just about to start.
Me	Look, that's not the issue! I don't even know what this *Code Geass* is!!
Y-ko	Well, Code Geass is...

a story about how this Lulu guy with a sister complex tries to do stuff!

	Does that make sense to you? Nice and simple, right?
Me	What the hell am I supposed to make sense out of?
Y-ko	Not enough? In that case, **read this and you'll get it!**
Me	...And what is this?

Y-ko   A dojinshi.

Me	Could you at least give me something officially sanctioned...?

I mean, if I cared whether this Lelouch was an uke or a seme,
that would help, but...

Y-ko	Oh and also, Lulu is very dedicated to his childhood sweetheart!
Me	I'm guessing I'd be better off not asking the

gender of this sweetheart...

And what happened to the topic of subprime loans?
Is it just me, or did we get way off track?

Y-ko	Don't worry about that.

...Oh, and since you have a stated fetish for cat ears, I have a question for you.

Me	At what point did I ever gain such a reputation?
Y-ko	Do these cat ears on Lulu work for you?

Me   Don't show me that!!

Y-ko   I thought you loved cat ears?

(continued)

ME, MY GIRLFRIEND, AND "MY GIRLFRIEND'S A GEEK." RETURNS

2008/01/29 08:51

It's been just four months since the release of Volume 1 of the comic adaptation of *My Girlfriend's a Geek*, in which I discovered a new personal characteristic: love of collarbones. Volume 2 now sits next to it on my bookshelf, which seems to proliferate with more and more manga by the day. Y-ko and I are filled with so many joys these days that it is hard to put it into words. To Shinba-*sensei* and the people at the publishing company for making our silly, stupid conversations into such a wonderful story and to the many fans who have supported this venture, thank you with all of my heart.

"Thank you so much."

......I lament the miserable state of my vocabulary, that after endless searching for the proper expression of the overflowing emotions within me, these were the best words I could come up with.

So.
Since I have again been given this space to use, I'd like to treat you all to a little status update by way of one of our patented goofy conversations.

Y-ko   Hey, I hear people raising this huge fuss about subprime loans every day. What exactly is the problem?

Me   Well, look who's invested in the real news for once in her life. It's a pretty complex subject. You still want to know?

Y-ko   I don't like complicated stuff.

Me   ...Then I'll make it simple.

Y-ko   Can you help me out by **explaining it in terms of *Gundam*?**

Me   **Explain it in terms of *Gundam*!?**
How do I do that!?

AFTERWORD ESSAY

PENTABU

P.79
TOPPING FROM BELOW KIND OF UKE - WHEN AN UKE PROPOSITIONS A SEME. THERE ARE MANY TYPES OF UKE: SCATTERBRAINED, CALCULATING, ETC.

P.80
BOYFRIEND-BUSTED - TO HAVE ONE'S BOYFRIEND DISCOVER ONE'S HOBBY. SOME GIRLS HIDE IT, LIKE MASA-NEE, BUT YUIKO-SAN WAS COMPLETELY OPEN ABOUT HER FUJOSHI NATURE TO TAIGA.

RECIPE FOR DISASTER - AN ABSOLUTE BRAWL OR BATTLE. ALSO REFERS TO THE STATE OF A MANGAKA'S STUDIO RIGHT BEFORE THE DEADLINE HITS.

REAL-LIFE B.L. - A RELATIONSHIP OR SITUATION THAT HAPPENS IN REAL LIFE WHICH SEEMS TO COME STRAIGHT OUT OF A BOYS' LOVE SCENARIO. BECAUSE BOTH MASA-NEE AND HER BOYFRIEND ARE THE SEME TYPE, ONE MIGHT SUGGEST THEIR RELATIONSHIP IS LIKE A LOVE AFFAIR BETWEEN TWO ALPHA MALES WHO NEVER BACK DOWN.

ELITE BUSINESSMEN - TALENTED, VALUABLE SALARYMEN. THEY CAN STRIKE BILLION-DOLLAR DEALS, MAKE FRIENDS WITH THE PRESIDENT, AND

IN SHORT...

...it's a school uniform café.

PILOT HELICOPTERS.

P.85
FIGHTER - A VIDEO GAME FEATURING PITCHED BATTLES BETWEEN TWO PLAYERS. THE FIERCE DRAMA BETWEEN MEN WHO USE THEIR BODIES TO CLASH VITALIZES THE IMAGINATION OF YOUNG LADIES.

P.90
HEAD OF THE STUDENT BODY - THE REPRE-SENTATIVE OF THE STUDENT CLASS, THE PERSON WHO OVERSEES ALL STUDENT COUNCIL ACTIVITY. TASTES ARE SPLIT BETWEEN THE ULTRA-SERI-OUS BESPECTACLED TYPE AND THE ULTRA-ALOOF SELFISH TYPE.

NEW STUDENT - WHETHER SEME OR UKE, IT'S THEIR BRILLIANT INNOCENCE THAT MAKES THEM GREAT. SOMETIMES IT'S THE BLUNT AND ANTISOCIAL NEW STUDENTS WHO ARE GREAT. TO REPHRASE, NEW STUDENTS ARE GREAT.

WHITE UNIFORM - WORN BY CHARISMATIC CHARACTERS IN A SPECIAL PRIVILEGED POSITION. KLUTZES WHO WOULD SPILL FOOD ON IT ARE NOT ALLOWED TO WEAR IT.

P.98
COVER ART - THE ILLUSTRATION THAT GRACES THE FRONT COVER OF A MANGA VOLUME. NOT ONLY DOES ONE GET TO SEE CHARACTERS IN COLOR FOR ONCE, BUT ONE ALSO FEELS ANTICI-PATION FOR THOSE CHARACTERS' ROLES WITHIN THE BOOK.

P.109
UKE PHEROMONES - TO EXUDE AN AIR OF BEING UKE. BRINGS ALL THE SEMES TO THE YARD.

P.112
MODEL READER - REFERS TO A MODEL WITHIN A FASHION MAGAZINE WHO IS INTRODUCED AS A READER OF THAT MAGAZINE. SOMETIMES REFERRED TO AS A "CELEBRITY READER."

P.140
COUPLING NOTATION - A DEPICTION OF A COUPLING OR PAIRING THAT REVEALS WHICH CHARACTER IS SEME AND WHICH IS UKE. OFTEN WRITTEN WITH AN "X" IN BETWEEN THE NAMES, BUT ALSO SHORTENED TO PARTS OF EACH NAME. (EX: SEBASxMILAN, SEBAMILA)

P.143
DREAMER - ONE WHO INSERTS HIM OR HERSELF INTO A STORY AND ENJOYS IMAGINING LOVE OR ADVENTURE WITH THE OTHER CHARACTERS. SOME WEBPAGES EVEN ALLOW YOU TO TYPE YOUR NAME AND THEN READ A STORY WITH THAT NAME INSERTED. A MARY SUE OR MARTY STU.

P.145
PERSONAL PAIRING - ONE'S PREFERRED PAIRING OR COUPLING.

WHAT THE HELL KIND OF WEIRD NARRATION DID SHE GIVE US?

WHAT IF SHE DECIDES KOUJI'S ONE OF THESE "MOE SEME" TYPES TOO?

IN WHICH CASE, SHE'S PROBABLY GOT SEME AND UKE ROLES DIVIDED UP FOR THE TWO OF US.

I CAN'T HELP BUT BE CURIOUS ABOUT THIS STUFF...

...BUT THERE'S NO WAY IN HELL I'LL EVER ASK!!

WHAT'S WRONG, TAIGA?

YOU'RE FROZEN STIFF, MAN.

AND THE MYSTERY OF THE "MOE SEME" DEEPENS...

MY GIRLFRIEND'S A GEEK VOLUME 2 ■ END ■

OH.

YOUR GIRLFRIEND'S HERE.

HEE

HEE

...SHE JUST MENTALLY OVERDUBBED SOME MORE CREEPY STUFF AT THE SIGHT OF US.

I HAVE A FEELING...

NOW EVEN MY INTERNAL DEFINITIONS OF SEME AND UKE ARE GROWING FUZZY.

I DON'T REALLY UNDERSTAND THE DIFFERENCE BETWEEN HER IDEA OF "MOE" AND "LOVE," FIRST OF ALL.

MILAN AS AN UKE? THAT'S KINDA MOE!

...WELL...

...I GUESS I'LL START BY CLEANING UP MY SCHOOL-RELATED STUFF.

THIS "SEPATAKU" NOVEL, MY FILM CLUB SCENARIO, MY HOMEWORK...

...AND NOW THIS ISSUE WITH MILAN-SAN.

TAIGA.

MY MIND JUST CAN'T KEEP UP WITH ALL OF THIS.

[Re] Black Ra...

Yuiko-san 10/23 22:36
[Re] Justice >o<)!

Yuiko-san 10/23 22:35
[Re] Oh man, crazy

Yuiko-san 10/23 22:33
[Re] Finally here!!

Yuiko-san 10/23 22:31
[Re] This week's SepaTaku

22:29
...een waiting!

ONE WEEK LATER...

...MY TEXT MESSAGES WITH YUIKO-SAN HAD BEEN COMPLETELY FILLED WITH HER THOUGHTS ON THE NEWEST CHARACTER IN "SEPATAKU."

HMMM...

WE'RE REALLY CLOSE, BUT IT FEELS LIKE A LONG-DISTANCE RELATIONSHIP.

ACTING AS A SEME? OR AS AN UKE?

WHAT, ARE YOU WONDERING ABOUT HIM?

KEH HEH HEH

IF I WAS CARELESS ENOUGH TO BRING UP THE TOPIC OF MILAN-SAN...

I'M WONDERING ABOUT HIM, ACTING AS YOUR BOYFRIEND!

144

DO I REALLY HAVE TO BE PRESENT FOR THIS CONVERSATION?

YES. LISTEN UP.

A BRAND-NEW MOE HAS JUST BEEN BROUGHT FORTH INTO THE WORLD.

HOW SAD IS MY LIFE RIGHT NOW, THAT I'M STANDING AROUND...

... LISTENING TO MY GIRLFRIEND FANTASIZE ABOUT POTENTIAL GAY ROMANTIC PARTNERS FOR ME?

[THINGS I FEEL SORRY ABOUT RIGHT NOW]
- ME AND MILAN, FOR BEING TURNED INTO B.L. MATERIAL
- ME AND MILAN, FOR NOT EVEN BEING CALLED BY OUR REAL NAMES
- THE INSIDE OF YUIKO-SAN'S HEAD, THAT SHE FINDS THIS STUFF FUN TO TALK ABOUT (AND ME, FOR HAVING TO PLAY ALONG)

UMM...

I HATE TO BE A PARTY POOPER, BUT...

ME? WELL, I'M NOT A DREAMER, SEE?

...WHY DO NONE OF THESE FANTASIES YOU HAVE EVER INCLUDE YOU?

RIGHT, RANGER?

YEAH!

THIS CONVERSATION IS ONLY GETTING WORSE AND WORSE!!

WHEN YOU LOOK AT IT THAT WAY, THERE'S PLENTY ABOUT HIM THAT'S KINDA HOT!

DON'T TALK TO YOUR DOLL, IT WON'T TALK BACK.

THAT'S PRETTY MUCH AN ORTHODOX PAIRING, RIGHT?

IN FACT, NOW THAT I THINK ABOUT IT, IT'S A PRETTY COMMONPLACE PATTERN.

A YOUNGER STUDENT SEME WITH AN ELITE SALARYMAN UKE.

UH...I WOULDN'T KNOW.

The Employment War of Love

B's Lovey

You were staring at me during the interview

An elite recruiter falls for young flesh

IT'S ALL COMING TOGETHER.

AS A MATTER OF FACT, I JUST READ A B.L. NOVEL WITH THAT SET-UP RECENTLY.

THOUGH IF WE'RE BEING HONEST, I THINK THE BOTH OF YOU ARE UKE...

SEBAMILA, HUH? YES, YES...

IT WAS IN THE NEWEST RELEASE FROM B'S-LOVEY'S LINE OF NOVELS.

HMM...

THAT'S THE FUTURE MOE SEME I KNOW AND LOVE!

GUU (THUMBS UP!)

YOU'RE A BABE!

BRAVO, SEBAS!!

I WISH YOU'D SHOW YOUR APPRECIATION BY STOPPING THE WHOLE "SEBAS" THING.

OF COURSE NOT!

I WISH YOU WOULD.

GREAT...SO YOU HAVEN'T FORGOTTEN ABOUT THAT...

HUH?

WAIT A MINUTE, WEREN'T YOU JUST SAYING SOMETHING ABOUT MILAN?

I CAN'T WAIT TO SEE WHAT KIND OF SEME YOU'LL TURN INTO! ☆

OH, WELCOME BACK!

OH. HE'S JUST AN EMPLOYEE.

OF COURSE.

THANK YOU SO MUCH. ♡

WELL, GOOD LUCK WITH THE GAME.

WELL, I'M GLAD TO HEAR IT.

NOW IT'S JUST A MATTER OF TIME BEFORE I SEIZE THE ONE I WANT!

OH, I JUST ASKED THE EMPLOYEE TO OPEN UP THE GAME AND REARRANGE THE ITEMS A BIT.

...WHAT WERE YOU DOING?

YUIKO-SAN...

YES, THAT'S IT! RIGHT THERE!

OH YEAH, BABY! COME ON, KAMEN RANGER!

SIGN: KAMEN RANGER

DAAAAAH! NOOOO!

KORORI (PLOP)

SORRY, SORRY. DON'T WORRY, I WAS LISTENING.

LET'S TRY ANOTHER ONE NOW. ♪

...AM I SUPPOSED TO BELIEVE THAT? ♪

GOTSU (THUD)

I WAS SO CLOOOSE!

S....

SEBAS...

プッ...
PUPU
(PFFT)

FINALLY, ALL OF MY TRAINING AND DISCIPLINE HAS PAID OFF!

I AM MOVED!!

WAIT, NO...

I'M PROUD OF YOU FOR TAKING THIS STEP.

HEH HEH HEH...

PLEASE, DON'T BE.

I WANT...

...TO BE A REALLY MOE SEME.

......

HUH?

WAIT, "MOE SEME" ...?

FUJOSHI NEWS vol.06

P.23
LIGHT NOVEL - SHORT JUVENILE NOVELS. STORIES ABOUT TEENAGE GIRLS WHO USE MAGIC AND PLOT TO TAKE OVER THE WORLD ARE POPULAR. TAIGA OWNS ONE EPIC FANTASY SERIES SET IN A WORLD BASED ON CHINESE MYTHOLOGY.

P.25
FIRST PRESS LIMITED EDITION - A VERSION OF A PRODUCT WITH SPECIAL EXTRAS THAT IS ONLY AVAILABLE IN THE FIRST ROUND OF PRODUCTION. WHEN THEY CONTAIN A TON OF EXTRA GOODIES, THE LIMITED NUMBERS CAN MAKE THEM HIGHLY COVETED AND HARD TO FIND.

SPECIAL DRAMA CD - A MINI-DRAMA IN WHICH THE VOICE ACTORS PLAY OUT A SCENARIO DIFFERENT FROM THE ORIGINAL STORY. LIKE A DREAM COME TRUE.

TRADING CARD - PUT IT IN YOUR TRAIN PASS CASE, AND YOU CAN CARRY YOUR FAVORITE CHARACTERS AROUND WITH YOU WHEREVER YOU GO.

STORE EXCLUSIVE - AN EXTRA BONUS THAT CAN ONLY BE OBTAINED AT A PARTICULAR STORE. BEING ABLE TO COLLECT ALL OF THESE IS PROOF OF LOVE AND WEALTH.

VOICE MESSAGE CD - CONTAINS MESSAGES FROM THE VOICE ACTORS IN A VARIETY OF SITUATIONS. FOR EXAMPLE, HELPING CELEBRATE YOUR BIRTHDAY, OR GENTLY WAKING YOU UP IN THE MORNING.

FULL COMPLETION - 100% MASTERY OF A COLLECTION. IN ADVENTURE GAMES, THIS MEANS UNLOCKING ALL OF THE STILLS IN THE GAME.

STILL - AN ILLUSTRATION WITHIN A GAME. USUALLY DEPICTING REALLY CHOICE AND JUICY SCENES, LIKE RUNNING INTO A GORGEOUS CELEBRITY AROUND A CORNER, OR HAVING HIM GIVE YOU A KISS THE MOMENT HE CATCHES THE HAT THAT GOT BLOWN OFF IN A GUST OF WIND.

P.33
FULLY-VOICED - WHEN ALL THE CHARACTER LINES IN THE ENTIRE GAME ARE SPOKEN ALOUD BY ACTORS.

THE MAN INSIDE - A PERSON WITH MULTIPLE PERSONALITIES. BUT IN THIS CASE, JUST A CHARACTER'S VOICE ACTOR.

P.38
BOBUGE - AN ABBREVIATION OF "BOYS' LOVE GAME" (BOIZU RABU GEMU). ALSO CALLED B.L.G. A POPULAR TERM, POSSIBLY BECAUSE THE SIMILARITY TO THE NAME "BOB" MAKES IT SOUND MANLY.

GIRL GAME - A GAME IN WHICH THE MAIN CHARACTER IS A GIRL.

P.57
B.L.CD - A BOYS LOVE DRAMA CD. AN AUDIO PRESENTATION OF A POPULAR COMIC OR NOVEL. LATELY, THERE ARE EVEN ORIGINAL DRAMA CDS. I WOULD LOVE TO HEAR A REAL B.L.CD OF TAIGA AND KOUJI OVER THE PHONE.

P.62
OTOME ROAD - A PARADISE FOR MAIDENS, RIGHT IN TOKYO'S OWN IKEBUKURO NEIGHBORHOOD. THE STREET IS LINED WITH ANIME AND DOJINSHI SHOPS, AND THERE ARE BUTLER CAFÉS CATERING TO B.L. FANS. A DIABOLICAL REALM WHICH A MAIDEN CAN ENTER AND NOT BE SEEN AGAIN FOR HALF A DAY, WHEN SHE EMERGES WITHOUT HALF OF HER SAVINGS.

P.71
SCHOOL UNIFORM CAFÉ - THE ULTIMATE IN SERVICE—A PLACE WHERE BOYS IN SCHOOL UNIFORMS WAIT ON YOUR EVERY NEED. AS OF APRIL 2008, THIS MAGICAL WONDERLAND DOES NOT YET EXIST.

P.76
EVENT - A GATHERING FOR DIRECT DOJINSHI BUYING AND SELLING. THEY COME IN MANY SHAPES AND SIZES, FROM MEGA-EVENTS LIKE SUMMER AND WINTER COMICKET, TO INFORMAL MEETINGS BASED AROUND INDIVIDUAL CHARACTER COUPLINGS.

ANTHROPOMORPHIC - A STORY IN WHICH A NON-HUMAN ANIMAL OR INANIMATE OBJECT IS TURNED INTO A PERSON AND TREATED AS A CHARACTER. AN EXERCISE IN MENTAL CREATIVITY IN WHICH TWO SUBWAY TRACKS OR A PENCIL AND ERASER CAN BE COUPLED.

HE IS SO OBNOXIOUS...

GATAN (THUMP)

...I'M NOT GONNA BE OUTDONE...

WHAT'S UP, SEBAS?

HMM?

I WANT...

...TO BE A REALLY MOE SEME.

WHAT!?

THE BOOKSTORE GUY (SEME)!!

BOOK: LOGICAL THINKING

← MOE BF

I GUESS YUIKO-SAN'S PROBABLY GETTING OFF WORK NOW.

I READ "SEPATAKU" VOLUME 2 THOROUGHLY.

I FEEL LIKE I'M GETTING A GOOD GRASP ON THE SERIES FOR THIS HIBITAKU NOVEL.

COME ON, YUIKO!

NO USE OVERTHINKING THIS NOW!

GREAT, THANKS.

IT'S FROM YAMAZAKI-SAN, THE DRESSMAKER.

I'LL SWITCH YOU OVER.

(CLICK)

PHONE CALL FOR KASHI-WABARA-SAN.

......

W.C.

YOU'VE GOT THE WHOLE "MILAN" PART NAILED, THOUGH.

YOU REALLY DO HATE HIM, DON'T YOU?

TSK!

SIT STRAIGHT, DWEEB.

WHY DOES MILAN ALWAYS HAVE TO SIT AT HIS DESK SIDEWAYS?

SEME, HUH...?

SHA
(FSHH)

FWA
(SWISH)

HAIR
FLIPPED
UP...

BASICALLY, ALL HIS SPECS SCREAM *MILAN*.

BOOK: LOGICAL THINKING

THE JERK KNOWS HIS COSMETICS, HE KNOWS HIS SWEETS, AND HE KNOWS HIS WORK.

I MEAN, I GUESS YOU COULD SAY HE'S A PLAYBOY.

HE MAKES ME SICK!

IT'S LIKE THE GUY'S A MODEL READER FOR SOME MEN'S FASHION MAGAZINE!

HIS SUITS, HIS BRIEFCASES, HIS VARIOUS ARTICLES—ALL AUTHENTIC ITALIAN, MORE SPECIFICALLY MILANESE.

THESE ARE...BAD THINGS?

THEY SOUND LIKE COMPLIMENTS TO ME.

I GUESS "MILAN" IS JUST A NICK-NAME...

TALL, LONG LEGS...

...ELEGANT AND SHAPELY...

...BEARING A COOL AND (NEEDLESSLY) FRIENDLY SMILE...

...WITH WHITE, SHINING TEETH.

...WEARING NICE, EXPENSIVE CLOTHES...

AS I SUSPECTED.

THAT'S SEME.

WE'RE SUPPOSED TO BE EXPANDING THE LINE OF PRODUCTS WE HANDLE NEXT YEAR...

...SO CORPORATE HQ SENT US THIS NEW BIGSHOT.

OH, YOU DON'T KNOW HIM. IT'S A GUY FROM THE COMPANY.

OH.

ACTUALLY... THAT KIND OF SOUNDS LIKE MILAN.

HUH?

THE CITY IN ITALY?

...SO, SPILL THE BEANS.

WAS THIS GUY FROM THE BOOKSTORE GOOD-LOOKING?

...YOU ARE WAY TOO INTERESTED IN THIS TOPIC.

OH, COME ONNN!

TWO PEOPLE REACHING FOR SUCH A BORING AND COMPLICATED BOOK AT THE SAME TIME?

THAT WOULD NEVER HAPPEN! SOME-THING'S FISHY!

ALL I'M SAYING IS, IT WAS AN AWKWARD WAY OF ACCEPTING THE BOOK, AND IT LEFT A WEIRD AFTERTASTE.

I WISH I COULD HAVE THANKED HIM PROPERLY.

THERE, SEE? YOU DO WANT TO GET HIS NUMBER!

THAT'S NOT WHAT I MEAN!

HEY, WHAT IF HE SLIPPED A BUSINESS CARD OR A ROSE INTO THE PAGES OF THE BOOK!?

......

HE DIDN'T LOOK LIKE A PARTY MAGICIAN TO ME.

TITLE: LOGICAL THINKING: IMPROVING YOUR LOGICAL SKILLS

HERE YOU ARE.

YOU WERE FIRST.

ロジカル・シンキング

ロジカル・シンキング α〜つ

ヾ〃キと〃G姫豎〜
〜〃〃ヾ〃口

SU (SHH)

NIKKORI (SMILE)

NO, PLEASE.

PARDON ME.

NO, IT'S ALL RIGHT!

IT'S ALL YOURS.

PARDON?

OKAY. WELL, WHY DON'T YOU HOLD ONTO IT FOR NOW?

HUH?

BYE!

KIRA (SPARKLE)

101

SHE'S BUYING THE BOOK ON THE RELEASE DAY, EVEN THOUGH SHE READ THE MAGAZINE AND KNOWS EXACTLY WHAT HAPPENED.

YUIKO-SAN?

SHE SURE LOVES THIS SERIES, I HAVE TO SAY.

WE JUST PASSED THE BOOKSTORE.

THE LINES GO TOO SLOWLY.

NO, WE'RE NOT GOING IN THAT ONE.

BOOK: SEPATTE TAKURO 2

EPI.08

My Girlfriend's a GEEK

THERE'S A DRAMA CD TOO, SO WE CAN—
I'LL PASS, THANKS.
WHAT? BUT IT'S A PERFECTLY FINE DRAMA! IT'S ABOUT A BATTLE TO THE END WITH A FATED RIVAL!
IT MIGHT NOT BE A B.L. CD, BUT HE STILL CRIES IN THAT LOVELY VOICE! YOU'RE MAKING A BIG MISTAKE!
CRIES?
...I CAN'T GO ALONG WITH THIS. YOUR FILTHY MOTIVES ARE SO COMPLETELY TRANSPARENT.
HEE HEE.
SEE, YUIKO? YOU INTRODUCED HIM TO THESE THINGS IN THE WRONG ORDER.
KON KON (KNOCK)
HI.
UM, EXCUSE ME.
?
I HAVE THE CHERRY PIE YOU ORDERED?
WE DIDN'T ORDER ANY PIE...

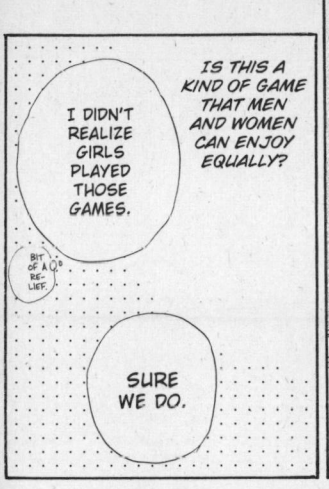

I DIDN'T REALIZE GIRLS PLAYED THOSE GAMES.

IS THIS A KIND OF GAME THAT MEN AND WOMEN CAN ENJOY EQUALLY?

BIT OF A RE-LIEF.

SURE WE DO.

I LIKE THAT ONE.

I KNOW WHAT SHE'S TALKING ABOUT.

OH YEAH...

WHOA.

OH, I'M NOT THAT SPECIAL.

THAT'S INTIMI- DATING.

THE FIGHT'S OVER IN SECONDS!

SHE JUST PILES ON ALL THE DEADLIEST ATTACKS. NO MERCY!

MASA-NEE'S BRILLIANT AT IT.

I JUST LIKE WATCHING OTHER PEOPLE PLAY.

YUIKO'S THE TYPE WHO ALWAYS USES MOVES SHE DOESN'T MEAN TO.

SHE'LL GET THE COMMANDS RIGHT ONE TIME IN THREE.

ARE YOU GOOD AT IT TOO, YUIKO-SAN?

KINDA BAD, ACTUALLY.

EH, NOT REALLY.

WHAT DO YOU MEAN?

THERE ARE PLENTY OF OTHER GOOD GAMES WITH BOKO IN THEM!

TELL YOU WHAT, SEBAS: I'LL BRING OVER A NICE, NORMAL PLAYSTATION GAME NEXT TIME.

WELL, HOW ABOUT THAT...

I GUESS I LEFT A GOOD FIRST IMPRESSION ON HER.

...AND THIS IS A...NORMAL... GAME THIS TIME, RIGHT?

OH, COME ON. DON'T SHRINK BACK LIKE THAT.

LOGO: BLOOD OF THE STARVING CAT

IT'S A POPULAR MULTIPLAYER 2-D FIGHTING GAME SERIES.

A FIGHTER ...?

IT'S A TOTALLY REGULAR OLD FIGHTING GAME.

SORRY. I CAN ONLY IMAGINE THAT GUY'S VOICE SAYING THE SAPPIEST LINES IN EXISTENCE.

GU (POKE)

WHAT'S THE BIG DEAL?

IT'S A COMPLIMENT OF THE HIGHEST ORDER!

ALL WE'RE SAYING IS THAT YOU SOUND LIKE A BIG-TIME FAMOUS VOICE ACTOR!

THIS ALL MAKES SENSE, THOUGH.

I REMEMBER THINKING YOU HAD A REALLY NICE VOICE THE VERY FIRST TIME WE MET...

HUH?

...I DID.

...YOU... YOU DID?

AFTER ALL, I SET YOUR PC TO BOKO MODE.

AH HA HA!

I STUCK "NOUVELLE MARIE" ON SEBAS'S COMPUTER. ♡

THAT'S SO CRUEL.

PFF!

HA (GASP)

MY PC....?

WHAT?

I....

...I HAVE TO DISAGREE. I DON'T SOUND LIKE HIM.

YES, YOU TOTALLY DO!

YOU THERE! STOP!

BIKU (FLINCH)

ERROR

AND SHE EVEN REPLACED ALL THE SYSTEM SOUNDS WITH HIS CREEPY LINES.

GIVE ME YOUR HAND, FLOWER PRINCESS.

I CONFESS I FEEL UNEASY WITHOUT ITS CONSTANT CARESS.

MAXIMILLIAN-SAMA

THEY'RE TALKING ABOUT HIM!!

HOW COULD I FORGET? SHE'S CLOGGING MY COMP WITH HER SAVE DATA.

SEBAS IS DOWN FOR THE COUNT.

GAKKURI (SLUMP)

UH-OH.

YOU AND YOUR BOYFRIEND ARE LIKE A REAL-LIFE B.L. RELATIONSHIP, MASA-NEE.

IF I GOT BOYFRIEND-BUSTED, IT'D BE A RECIPE FOR DISASTER.

YOU'RE SO LUCKY, YUIKO.

YEAH, ONE WHERE BOTH OF YOU ARE SEME.

LIKE TWO ELITE BUSINESSMEN.

PIKU (TWITCH)

YOUR SEBAS-KUN IS REALLY UNDERSTANDING.

I WISH I HAD A SEBAS-KUN.

MY NAME IS NOT SEBAS...

MUKURI (RISE)

SEBAS IS BACK FOR MORE.

AHA.

DA HA HA!

THIS IS THE WEIRDEST GOSSIP I'VE EVER HEARD.

IT'S BRILLIANT!

AND DAISY IS THE HONEST AND COOL TYPE.

NO, REALLY? WHAT OF!?

AFTER DISCOVERING THIS ONE, I'M DETERMINED TO MAKE MY NEXT PROJECT AN ANTHRO-POMORPHIZED ONE.

DANDELION SEME.

. . .

HE SPENDS EVERY DAY OOZING WHITE SAP FROM HIS STEM AS HE THINKS OF DAISY...

HE'S LIKE A PRETTY BOY IN A SMALL TOWN.

DANDELION WANTS TO CROSS THAT LINE WITH HIS CHILDHOOD FRIEND, DAISY.

THICK WHITE SAP.

KON (KNOCK)

KON

I SENSE DANGER!

I AM SURROUNDED BY THESE DARK JEDI OF THE FUJOSHI WORLD! TRAPPED!!

EXCUSE ME.

NO, THEY DON'T.

SOME EVEN CALL THIS SKILL "THE MIND'S EYE"!

SO ALL THAT STUFF YOU WERE EXPOUNDING UPON WAS JUST WHAT YOU WISH YOU COULD DO...?

SO DO I...

GOSH, I WISH I HAD THAT SKILL...

POWAWAAA (LAH-LAH)

FUJOSHI IDEALS

I ALWAYS CRY WHEN THE ARTIST I LIKE ONLY DREW THE COVER AND HER COLLABORATORS DID THE INSIDE.

OF COURSE, WHEN THE RATIO OF HITS IS SUPER-LOW, IT PUTS A REAL DAMPER ON THINGS.

[Y]

BUY AS MANY AS POSSIBLE, AND YOU'RE BOUND TO STRIKE GOLD EVENTUALLY!

AND PICKING OUT STUFF AT RANDOM CAN REALLY SQUEEZE A BUDGET.

[S]

BIKU (CLINCH)

GU (CLENCH)

SNUG ✨

IN A BAG

BUT IT'S ALWAYS A GAMBLE WHEN YOU TAKE ON A SHRINK-WRAPPED BOOK OR SOMETHING YOU HAVEN'T SEEN BEFORE.

...

BISHI (JAB)

I... SEE...

WHAT YOU NEED IN THAT CASE IS...

...THE ABILITY TO JUDGE THE INSIDE OF THE BOOK BY ITS COVER.

THAT'S THE KEY.

YUI-CHAN HAS SUCH A MANLY WAY OF BUYING STUFF.

ARTISAN, RIGHT.

IT'S LIKE THE SKILL OF AN ARTISAN OR SOMETHING!

WHAT WOULD YOU CALL THAT?

GAZE UPON THE TRUTH WITH UNCLOUDED EYE, AND MAKE YOUR DECISION!!

真の
萌本

A TRUE MOE BOOK

YOU CAN'T BE FOOLED BY A BOOK IN WHICH ALL THE WORK WENT INTO THE COVER!

NO KIDDING! THIS STUFF WAS A LOT OF WORK TO PICK OUT!

Go on, take a look! ♡

HOW CAN YOU HAVE SO MANY!?

ARE THOSE ALL BOOKS!?

NO WONDER YOUR BAG WAS SO DAMN HEAVY! YOU BOUGHT A MILLION THINGS!

EVEN THE ONES THAT HAVE SAMPLES ARE JUST A SINGLE PAGE.

AND ALL THESE THINGS ARE PACKED IN PLASTIC BAGS, SO YOU CAN'T SEE WHAT THEY'RE LIKE.

EXTRA MATERIAL! ADDED DETAILS! REDRAWINGS! AFTERWORDS!

AND HAVING A COPY ON HAND FOR PERPETUITY!

THE BENEFITS ARE MYRIAD!!

AT LEAST WHEN I BUY THE VOLUMES OF MANGA I READ IN MAGAZINES, I ALREADY KNOW WHAT I'M GETTING.

HUH?

S-SORRY...

WHY NOT JUST PICK ONE?

YOU BUY THE MAGAZINES AND THEN THE VOLUMES LATER?

(B)OYS (L)OVE (T)HROBBING?

(B)OYS (L)OVE (T)HRILLS!

(B)OYS (L)OVE (T)ESTI—

A B.L.T. SANDWICH!

AHA! THIS IS IT!

WHAT SHOULD WE ORDER?

OOH, NICE!

I HEAR PRETTY MUCH EVERYTHING IS GOOD HERE.

MENU: PASTRY BREAD

だっはっは

DA-HA-HA-HA!

SOME-ONE... SAVE ME!!

VERY GOOD OF YOU TO ASK!

OH!

WHAT DID YOU GET TODAY, YUI-CHAN?

WELL, LET'S ORDER.

PAKA (THWUP)

I PULLED IN A MAJOR HAUL!

TA-DAA! ♥

!

PINPON (DING-DONG) PANPON.

WAITER BELL

THIS IS A SECRET GARDEN, A HIDDEN PARADISE UNREACHABLE EXCEPT BY RESERVATION.

"Blue Labial Academy."

IN SHORT...

...it's a school uniform café.

...LIKE WHAT THE SCHOOL CLASS DOES DURING CULTURE FESTIVALS?

KYA!

MASA-NEE'S ALWAYS GOT AN EAR TO THE GROUND. UNIFORMS!

HEH! LET'S JUST SAY I'VE GOT CONNEC-TIONS.

I'M AMAZED YOU GOT RESER-VATIONS!

I'VE BEEN CURIOUS ABOUT THIS PLACE SINCE BEFORE IT OPENED.

KYA!

CAN YOU PICK A SCENARIO WHEN YOU RESERVE A TABLE?

WELCOME, SENPAI!

ARMBAND: STUDENT COUNCIL

!!?

SIGN: STUDENT COUNCIL

I AM.

YOU'RE PROBABLY WONDERING, "WHAT THE HECK IS THIS PLACE?"

THE STUDENT COUNCIL IS HOLDING A MEETING TODAY, AS YOU KNOW.

THIS ROOM'S POPULAR.

UH...

EEK, STUDENT COUNCIL!

BETTER SEND HER A MESSAGE, TELL HER TO CALL ME WHEN SHE'S DONE.

PAKO (THWUP)

WELL...

...MIGHT AS WELL TAKE SHELTER IN A NEARBY STORE.

HUH?

SHE ALREADY SENT ME SOMETHING...

SIGN: SWEETS SALE

"OH CRAP, IT'S A TREASURE TROVE."

SHE WAS SO EXCITED, SHE DIDN'T EVEN HAVE TIME TO PUT IN A SMILEY EMOTICON.

PACHIN (SNAP)

I WISH SHE HAD BEEN CONSIDERATE FROM THE START...

...AND CHOSEN NOT TO DRAG ME ALONG AT ALL...

YOU JUST WAIT HERE! ♪

I'M NOT CRUEL ENOUGH TO MAKE YOU COME INSIDE.

THIS'S A BATTLE-GROUND FOR GIRLS.

I'LL BE BACK IN A SNAP! ♥

SIGN:
OF THE GIRLS, BY THE GIRLS, FOR THE GIRLS

CHIRA (PEEK)

......

乙女の
乙女による
乙女の為の

I'M SORRY, YUIKO-SAN!

DA (DASH)

THIS IS SOME KIND OF KINKY HUMILIATION GAME!?

I JUST CAN'T DO THIS!!

B-BOOK

池袋本店

1F.CD.同人誌
2F.同人誌買取
3F.CD.グッズ買

同人誌高価買

SIGN: B-BOOKS
IKEBUKURO STORE
1F: CDS, DOJINSHI
2F: DOJINSHI PURCHASE
3F: CDS & GOODS
WE BUY USED DOJINSHI!

THIS IS HOSTILE TERRITORY.

IT'S AN AWAY GAME.

TODAY'S DATE WAS SUPPOSED TO BE SHOPPING AND A TRIP TO THE AQUARIUM.

BUT...

HEY, SEBAS, I JUST REALIZED SOMETHING.

I JUST WANNA GO HOME...!

WE'RE ACTUALLY NOT FAR FROM OTOME ROAD! ♥

FU CHIMPU

I THOUGHT THIS WAS SUPPOSED TO BE A BUSINESS PARK!

"MAIDEN" ROAD? SEEMS LIKE IT OUGHT TO BE MORE INNOCENT AND PURE...

AND WHAT'S WITH THE NAME, "OTOME ROAD"?

WHEN THE HELL DID IT TURN INTO FUJOSHI ALLEY...?

NO! STOP!

WHOSE IDEA WAS THAT?

DON'T THINK ABOUT IT! IT'LL ONLY LEAD TO DEFEAT.

FUJOSHI NEWS

IT'S HUMILIATING IN MORE WAYS THAN ONE...!!

I CAN'T BELIEVE THIS IS BEING REVEALED.

YUIKO-SAN'S BEEN FORCING TAIGA TO WRITE HER A B.L. STORY BASED ON "SEPATTE TAKURO." AT FIRST HE COMPLAINED, BUT HE SEEMS TO BE ENJOYING IT MORE AND MORE LATELY! LET'S TAKE A LOOK AT THE THREE DIFFERENT VERSIONS OF THE SAMPLE SCENE HE MENTIONED IN THE LAST CHAPTER! ♥

[NORMAL]

"AREN'T YOU COLD, TAKURO?"

"I-I'M FINE."

TAKURO HEARD THE NERVOUS STRAIN IN HIS OWN VOICE AND FELT HIS CHEEKS FLUSH.

HE HOPED THE SUN SETTING ACROSS THE HORIZON WOULD HIDE THE REDDENING.

HE WAS ALONE WITH HIBINO ON A LONELY STRETCH OF THE BEACH.

ALL THAT COULD BE HEARD WAS THE GENTLE LAPPING OF THE WAVES.

AFRAID THAT HIBINO WOULD SOMEHOW HEAR THE RAGING POUNDING WITHIN HIS CHEST, TAKURO SHOOK HIMSELF.

"WHAT'S UP?"

"UMM, N-NOTHING!"

"YOU'RE SO WEIRD."

HIBINO GIGGLED AND LOOKED AT TAKURO.

HIS KIND, CARING GAZE WAS SO DIRECT, TAKURO COULDN'T HELP BUT STARE BACK INTO HIBINO'S EYES.

"TAKURO..."

"C-CAPTAIN..."

A LONG SILENCE FOLLOWED. DURING THAT MOMENT, A BEAM OF LIGHT FROM THE SETTING SUN FELL UPON TAKURO, WHILE HIBINO SLOWLY APPROACHED.

......OH! HE'S GOING TO KISS ME......

[LITERARY]

THE GREAT ORB, NOW RIPENED TO A DEEP MANDARIN, SUNK BENEATH THE HORIZON.

EVEN THE PALE WATER THAT FLOODED THE FOOTSTEPS HIBINO AND TAKURO LEFT IN THEIR WAKE WERE GLISTENING GOLDEN AMBER.

"TURN TO ME, TAKURO."

HIBINO REACHED OUT HIS FINGERTIPS TO TRACE TAKURO'S SILENT CHEEK, HIS GAZE BORING DEEP INTO THE BOY'S PUPILS.

"WHAT IS IT, CAPTAIN?"

HIS WIDE, INNOCENT EYES GRIPPED HIBINO, VOID OF ANY FEAR.

"WOULD YOU LIKE TO SHARE A KISS, TAKURO?"

"HUH? WHAT DID YOU SAY?"

[TEXT MESSAGE]

AN ORANGE SUNSET.

WE STOOD AND WATCHED IT SINK.

THE CAPTAIN AND I.

WE SLOWLY REALIZED OUR DISTANCE.

OUR HANDS TOUCHED.

"WHOOPS."

"SORRY."

WE BOTH APOLOGIZED.

IT WAS SO STRANGE AND FUNNY.

WE BOTH LAUGHED.

THEN, THE CAPTAIN DREW ME INTO HIS ARMS.

HE KISSED ME.

IT WAS MY FIRST EVER KISS.

ALSO...YOU MIGHT WANT TO FLESH OUT THE DESCRIPTION OF THE SUNSET A BIT MORE.

...I THINK THE NORMAL VERSION WORKS BEST, PERSONALLY.

HUH? HUH? YOU SAW IT, DIDN'T YOU? YOU READ THE ENTIRE PAGE I HAD LEFT OPEN, KOUJI? WITH THE CHARACTERS "TAKURO" AND "CAPTAIN," STRAIGHT OUT OF A MANGA, TALKING ABOUT KISSING AND SO ON? YOU READ THAT WHOLE THING, DIDN'T YOU? AND THAT'S IT? THAT'S YOUR WHOLE REACTION? REALLY?

SURE.

TH-THANKS FOR THE ADVICE.

YOU THINK SO?!

THIS IS WAY TOO HIGH-LEVEL, MAN!

IS THIS SUPPOSED TO BE SOME KIND OF SUBLIMINAL MENTAL TEST?

I'M RECEIVING MESSAGES!

AND SURE ENOUGH, I COULD FEEL THE WAVES EMANATING FROM KOUJI'S JAPANESE TRANSLATION.

KOU-JIIIIII!!!

Kouji!! Don't look at that!

DOTATA (STOMP)

What is this?

Well, I already saw it.

I can't tell you!!

You can touch it, but don't look! Close the window!

NO, WAIT! I HAVEN'T SAVED IT YET!

Don't look? But

DOTA (STOMP)

SHE'S LAUGHING!

Ah-ha-ha-ha-ha-ha-ha!!

Y...

I DIDN'T WANT YOU TO HEAR THAT...

YUIKO-SAN...

I'M SO SORRY...

KOUJI'S ENGROSSED IN HIS TRANSLATION.

GUESS I CAN TAKE THIS MOMENT TO GET IN A LITTLE "SEPATAKU" WORK.

LET'S SEE HERE...

UMM...

HOW FAR DID I GET?

"WHAT IS IT, CAPTAIN?" HIS INNOCENT PUPILS SIMPLY HELD HI EINO, VOID OF ANY FEAR. "WOULD YOU LIKE TO SHARE A KISS, TAKURO?" "HUH? WHAT DID YOU SAY?"

"TAKURO..." "C-CAPTAIN..." A LONG SILENCE FOLLOWED, IN THAT MOMENT, A BEAM OF LIGHT FROM THE SETTING SUN FELL UPON TAKURO. .....OH! HE'S GOING TO KISS ME......

IT WAS SO STRANGE AND FUNNY. WE BOTH LAUGHED. THEN THE CAPTAIN DREW ME INTO HIS ARMS. HE KISSED ME. IT WAS MY FIRST EVER KISS.

I WAS SO CONFUSED ABOUT THE WHOLE THING, I WROTE UP THREE DIFFERENT VERSIONS OF THE SCENE.

THE KISS SCENE...!!

OH YEAH...

IN NORMAL WRITING, IN LITERARY PROSE, AND IN SHORT TEXT MESSAGE STYLE.

I GIVE UP.

MMMMM...

MANAGED TO FINISH, THOUGH I DON'T KNOW HOW...

TATATATATA (CLACK)

TATATATATA

AAAAAAAA

AAAAAAAA

HEY, KOUJ—

OOPS.

sepaaku novel.txt

Text document (*.txt)

ANSI

KACHI (CLICK)

Open (0)

Cancel

WHAT'S UP WITH YOU?

DOES THAT STUFF FREAK YOU OUT ENOUGH TO MAKE YOU SICK?

YOU'RE COVERING YOUR MOUTH.

N-NO, THAT'S NOT IT.

FREAK ME OUT?

I'VE GOT A HALF-WRITTEN B.L. NOVEL ON THIS COMPUTER AS WE SPEAK, FOR GOD'S SAKE!

DEAR "SEPATAKU" AUTHOR, I AM SO, SO SORRY ABOUT THIS.

SPEAKING OF WHICH, I'M STUCK IN THE MIDDLE OF IT NOW.

JUST TELL ME WHEN YOU DO, SO I CAN TAKE PICTURES.

IF YOU CHEAT ON ME WITH KOUJI-KUN, I'LL HAVE TO PUNISH YOU!

OH...

DON'T ASK WHY— JUST ACCEPT THE APOLOGY...

HUH?

BY THE WAY, I'M SORRY.

FINISHED WITH MY VOCABULARY TRANSLATION.

HERE WE GO...

SOMETIMES YOU CAN PRACTICALLY FEEL THE PHANTOM PULSE OF HIS OVERLY-SARCASTIC SENTENCES EMANATING FROM A DISTANCE.

USUALLY WHEN YOU OFFER FLATTERING PRAISE IN A LITERARY WAY, IT GOES...

"YOU" ARE "BEAUTIFUL"... "YOUNG"...

THESE EXAMPLES ARE SUPPOSED TO FALL UNDER OBSEQUIOUS FAWNING, I GUESS.

A STARRY SKY, THE SEA AT NIGHT...

FORM... SHADOW...

BEAUTY...

A GODDESS WITH CLEAR, PURE EYES...

...SOMETHING ABOUT THE LIGHT OF THE SUN.

WAIT, THE OBJECT IN THIS SENTENCE IS A "HIM"...

HUH?

KOUJI?

GI (CREAK)

UH-OH, KOUJI'S IN STORY-TELLER MODE...

KOOOO (FWOOM)

IT'S JUST A SIMPLE HOMEWORK ASSIGNMENT.

HEY, MAN.

DON'T GET TOO INVESTED IN THIS THING.

YEAH...

FUJOSHI NEWS

WHAT'S THIS "DREAMING NOUVELLE MARIE" GAME SERIES THAT YUIKO-SAN'S COMPLETELY NUTS OVER THESE DAYS? READ ON AND FIND OUT! ♥

BY THE WAY, THIS GAME DOES NOT EXIST. DON'T BOTHER YOUR LOCAL GAME SHOP EMPLOYEES ABOUT IT! ♡

SUMMARY

I'm Mari Hanabishi, and I used to be a normal girl...until one day I woke up and found that I was the princess of another world! And, all of a sudden, a whole gang of studly princes wanted my hand in marriage... What's a single girl to do?

A LOVE SIMULATION GAME POPULAR WITH GIRLS THESE DAYS. AS YOU CAN IMAGINE, THE GAME'S THEME IS "MARRIAGE." THE MAIN CHARACTER IS A POTENTIAL BRIDE FOR A NUMBER OF PRINCES AND CAN MARRY WHICHEVER PRINCE SHE GAINS THE MOST POINTS WITH IN THE LIMITED TIME THEY SHARE TOGETHER. THE PLAYER CAN, OF COURSE, BECOME THE QUEEN OF THIS FANTASY WORLD, BUT THE SECRET BEST ENDING INVOLVES GOING BACK TO OUR REGULAR WORLD AND FINDING OUT THAT THE CHOSEN PRINCE HAS TRANSFERRED TO THE MAIN CHARACTER'S SCHOOL. YUIKO-SAN'S FAVORITE CHARACTER IS MAXIMILLIAN (VOICED BY AKIRA KUROKAWA—SEE P.81.)

OUR MAIN CHARACTERS, COSPLAYING AS MARI HANABISHI AND MAXIMILLIAN. HOW ROMANTIC! ♥

BIKU (FLINCH)

YOU THERE! STOP!

ERROR

OF—

...I WANTED TO COME OVER AND SEE YOUR PLACE!

...IS THAT A BAD THING?

OF COURSE NOT.

IT'S PERFECTLY FINE.

YOU'RE WELCOME TO COME TO MY HOUSE ANY TIME YOU WANT...

'KAY.

*PISTA SOFTWARE WILL NOT RUN IN XD.

LONG LIVE PRINCE MAXIMILLIAN! ♡♡

MUGYU (SMUSH)

WHAAAT!?

OF COURSE! IT'S FULLY-VOICED.

THAT'S STANDARD STUFF THESE DAYS!

THE GAME... TALKS.

FLOWER FAIRY?

OH MAXIMILLIAN, I LOVE YOU, BOTH THE MAN INSIDE AND OUT. ♡

NOW THAT I THINK OF IT...

...THE WHOLE GAME SCENARIO ISN'T THAT MUCH BETTER THAN MY STUPID WISHFUL THINKING A MOMENT AGO...

BETTER NOT SAY THAT OUT LOUD, IF I VALUE MY LIFE.

IT WAS THE ONLY FLAW OVERALL.

YOU'RE A HARD SELL.

I JUST COULDN'T GET OVER HOW STUPID AND CORNY THAT GUY'S LINES WERE...

IT'S ESPECIALLY WEIRD SINCE SHE SAID...

...AFTER THE MOVIE WE SAW LAST TIME.

BOOK: PROGRAM

CONGRATS, BUD.

YOU'VE MASTERED THE ABILITY TO DETECT YOUR GIRLFRIEND'S TASTE IN (TWO-DIMENSIONAL) MEN!

コフォォ フォォォ・・・
KOFOOOOO (PFFFFF)

MIND IF I HAVE A DONUT?

YEAH, EAT UP.

UH, DON'T FORGET ABOUT YOUR COFFEE.

DON'T WANT IT TO GET COLD, Y'KNOW?

YEAH. THANKS.

Mari Hanabishi is a totally normal girl... until the day when she accidentally gets sucked into another world!

In this new land, gorgeous princes visit in search of a bride.♡ Accept the blessing of the goddess of dreams and snag that beau!

~From the packaging~

......

YAHOOOOO!

SHE'S NUTS OVER THIS THING. WHAT KIND OF GAME IS IT, ANYWAY?

IT LOOKS LIKE A GIRL ON THE PACKAGING, SO I'M GUESSING IT'S NOT B.L., AT THE VERY LEAST.

Eternal Sweet Romance Series
"Dreaming Nouvelle Marie"

Dreaming Nouvelle Marie

WELL, ENOUGH ABOUT BOOKS FOR NOW.

COME!

SO, UMM... WHAT DID YOU WANT TO DO WITH IT?

WRITE A PAPER? EDIT SOME PHOTOS?

IT IS TIME FOR THE COMPUTER, SEBAS!!

OH, RIGHT.

SFX: GOSO (RUSTLE) GOSO

A GAME. ♡

YES?

ON THE OTHER HAND...

KYORO (GLANCE) KYORO

HERE YOU GO.

WELL, THANKS.

I ASSUME THAT WAS MEANT AS A COMPLIMENT?

I FIGURED YOU'D HAVE THE PLACE IN TIP-TOP SHAPE, SINCE YOU'RE SO ANAL AND ALL.

...ANY MANGA IN THIS ROOM.

DID YOU HIDE IT?

I'M NOT SEEING...

ARE YOU SERIOUS!?

WELL, THAT'S BECAUSE I DON'T REALLY READ ANY.

THOUGH I DID BUY "SEPATAKU" RECENTLY.

OH.

SHELF: DOJINSHI

ABSOLUTELY!!

KOTO
(THUNK)

WELL,
THERE
GOES MY
SUNDAY! ♪

THIS
SHOULD
BE FUN!
♡

BACK
TO THE
GAME.

KACHI
(CLICK)

ACK!

▷ Oh fine. I'll go.

▷ Not right now...

PIHO
(BLIP)

HEE
HEE!

That's fine!
I'll make sure
to clean up.

16

Help me, Sebas!

PAKU (STARE?)

My dear, faithful compy has finally gone to heaven~ which sucks, because I really need to do something~!

...

SO HER COMPUTER JUST DIED, HUH?

OH, FANTASTIC! SHE'S REALLY HIT THE GROUND RUNNING WITH THIS WHOLE "SEBAS" THING.

FINE, FINE. SEBAS IT IS.

PAKA (THWUP)

KACHA (KCHAK)
I JUST BOUGHT A BRAND NEW LAPTOP, AND THE FIRST TWO THINGS I DO ON IT ARE WRITE A COLLEGE PAPER AND A B.L. STORY...
URGH...
DON'T GET DOWN ON ME, PARTNER. LET'S FIND A WAY THROUGH THIS TOGETHER...!
YOU BET!
TOPOPO (GLUG)
PIPIPI (BEEP)
PIPIPI
MM?
THAT'S THE RINGTONE FOR A MESSAGE FROM YUIKO-SAN!
PAKA (THWUP)
COMING, MY DEAR!
PIPIPIRURU

SO FAR, SO GOOD...

IT'S WHAT COMES NEXT THAT'S THE REAL BATTLE.

HOW TO GET LOVE TO BLOSSOM BETWEEN TAKURO AND THE CAPTAIN...

YOU'RE THE MOST BEAUTIFUL CREATURE IN THE WORLD.

TAKURO...

CAPTAIN...

HA-HA! CATCH ME IF YOU CAN!

WAIT, YOU LITTLE SCAMP!

TAKURO!

↑ THIS TYPE →

PLUS, I'M PRETTY SURE THIS TYPE OF SCENE ISN'T EXACTLY WHAT YUIKO-SAN WANTS FROM ME.

BETTER CHECK THAT MEMO SHE SENT ME!

CAN'T HELP BUT WONDER.

BUT WHY ARE THEY FALLING IN LOVE? THAT'S THE PROBLEM...

I MEAN, THIS IS A COLOSSAL STRETCH ANY WAY YOU CUT IT...

KUUU (GUHH)

IT'S THE RETURN OF THE ETERNALLY SWEET ROMANCE GAME SERIES FOR GIRLS!! THE HEROINE APPEARS, DECKED OUT IN "DREAMING NOUVELLE MARIE" COSPLAY! ♡
*THIS GAME SERIES IS FICTIONAL.
EP1.05
My Girlfriend's a GEEK

CONTENTS

VOLUME 1 BREAKDOWN

My Girlfriend's a GEEK

AT A GLANCE

♥THE STORY SO FAR♥

Taiga Mutou fell in love with his new coworker, Yuiko Ameya-san, at first sight. He summoned his courage to ask her out, and she said yes! "But you understand that I'm a *fujoshi*, right?" Taiga, not understanding what a "*fujoshi*" is, says, "That's fine!!" Originally elated with his new relationship, Taiga slowly begins to understand Yuiko-san's *fujoshi* personality. The first thing she does is give him the nickname "Sebas" because he "seems like a butler"! What's going to happen in this relationship fraught with trouble ahead (mostly for Taiga)!?

YUIKO AMEYA

An office worker in her third year at the company. Her typing is rapid and powerful. Her favorite manga is *Sepatte Takuro*, running in *Weekly Shonen Step*.

TAIGA MUTOU

A normal college student. He wears glasses, but only during class. The kind of guy who seems incompetent, but gets things done when it comes down to it.

KOUJI

Taiga's friend and companion since high school. The cool and dedicated older brother type.

My Girlfriend's a GEEK

2

RIZE SHINBA
STORY: PENTABU